3 USES OF THE KNIFE

The Columbia Lectures on American Culture

3 USES OF THE KNIFE

on the nature and purpose of drama

David Mamet

Columbia University Press   New York

Columbia University Press
Publishers Since 1893
New York   Chichester, West Sussex
Copyright © 1998 David Mamet

Library of Congress Cataloging-in-Publication Data
Mamet, David.
    Three uses of the knife : on the nature and purpose of drama /
David Mamet.
        p.   cm.
    Includes index.
    ISBN 978-0-231-11088-4 (alk. paper)
    1. Drama. 2. Drama—Technique.   3. Arts.   I. Title.
    PN1620.A1M36   1998
    808.2—dc21

                                                    97-23606

Casebound editions of Columbia University Press books are printed
on permanent and durable acid-free paper.
Printed in the United States of America
Designed by Linda Secondari
c 10 9 8 7 6 5 4 3

*The Press acknowledges with thanks a Centennial gift from Lydia and John
Moore toward the costs of publishing this book.*

This book is dedicated to Michael Feingold.

CONTENTS

3 USES
OF THE
KNIFE

CHAPTER ONE
THE WIND-CHILL FACTOR

It is in our nature to dramatize. At least once a day we reinterpret the weather—an essentially impersonal phenomenon—into an expression of our current view of the universe: "Great. It's raining. Just when I'm blue. Isn't that just like life?"

Or we say: "I can't remember when it was this cold," in order to forge a bond with our contemporaries. Or we say: "When I was a lad the winters were longer," in order to avail ourselves of one of the delights of aging.

The weather is impersonal, and we both understand it and exploit it as dramatic, i.e., having a plot, in order to understand its meaning *for the hero*, which is to say for ourselves.

We dramatize the weather, the traffic, and other impersonal phenomena by employing exaggeration, ironic juxtaposition, inversion, projection, all the tools the dramatist uses to create, and the psychoanalyst uses to interpret, emotionally significant phenomena.

We dramatize an incident by taking events and reordering them, elongating them, compressing them, so that we understand their personal meaning to us—to us as the protagonist of the individual drama we understand our life to be.

If you said, "I waited at the bus stop today," that probably wouldn't be dramatic. If you said, "I waited at the bus stop for a long time today," that might be a little more dramatic. If you said, "The bus came quickly today," that wouldn't be dramatic (and there would really be no reason to say it). But you might say, "Do you know how quickly that bus came today?"—and all of a sudden, we're taking the events of life and using dramatic tools.

"I waited *half an hour* for a bus today" is a dramatic statement. It means: "I waited that amount of time sufficient for me to be sure you will understand it was 'too long.'"

(And this is a fine distinction, for the utterer cannot pick a time too short to be certain that understanding is communicated, or too long for the hearer to accept it as appropriate—at which point it becomes not *drama* but *farce*. So the *ur*-dramatist picks unconsciously, and perfectly, as it is our nature to do, the amount of time that

allows the hearer to *suspend his or her disbelief*—to *accept*
that the half-hour wait is not outside the realm of prob-
ability, yet *is* within the parameters of the unusual. The
hearer then accepts the assertion for the enjoyment it
affords, and a small but perfectly recognizable play has
been staged and appreciated.)

"This is only the third time in NFL history a rookie
previously benched with what was believed to be a seri-
ous injury returned to rush for more than 100 yards in
a post-season game."

That NFL statistic, like the wait for the bus, takes the
unremarkable and frames it to afford dramatic enjoyment. The ejaculation "What a run!" is given a statistic
to allow us to savor it better/longer/differently. That
run is assigned the dramatic weight of the incontrovert-
ible.

Take the useful phrases "you always" and "you
never." In these we reformulate the inchoate into the
dramatic. We exploit the utterance and give it dramatic
form, for some personal benefit. We might gain tran-
scendence over our significant other, as in the case of
"you always" and "you never." We might open a dinner
table chat with a nice topic of conversation: "I waited
half an hour for a bus today."

In these small plays we make the general or the unremarkable particular and objective, i.e., part of a universe

our very formulation proclaims understandable. It's good dramaturgy.

Bad dramaturgy can be found in the palaver of politicians who have somewhere between nothing much and nothing to say. They traduce the process and speak, rather, of the subjective and nebulous: they speak of the Future. They speak of Tomorrow, they speak of the American Way, Our Mission, Progress, Change.

These are mildly or less mildly inflammatory terms (they mean "Rise Up," or "Rise Up and Rush Around Boldly") that *stand in* for drama. They are placeholders in the dramatic progression, and they function similarly to sex scenes or car chases in a trash film—they are related to no real problem and are inserted as modular treats in a story devoid of content.

(We may assume, similarly, that as Democrats and Republicans respond to each other's positions by screaming "scandal," their positions are essentially identical.)

We can see the natural dramatic urge in newspaper quotes of a film's grosses. The dramatic urge—our impulse to structure cause and effect in order to increase our store of practical knowledge about the universe—is absent in the film itself, but emerges spontaneously in our proclamation of a naturally occurring drama *between* films. Just as, when we have exhausted our interest in Zeus, we spontaneously create the pantheon.

Some say the land is growing hotter. No, say the others, it is not, and your senses are at fault. And, so, we have the wind-chill factor. Since we cannot wish away our anxiety about climate change, we dramatize it, transforming even that (one would think) least personal, most scientific measurement, the temperature, exactly as we dramatized our wait at the bus stop.

I need to feel maligned, so I say, "And the damn bus was One Half Hour Late!" I need to feel other than anxious, so I say, "The temperature may be hotter than normal—but, *with* the wind-chill factor . . ."

(Please note that this "factor" is a rather elegant dramatic device, for the wind does not blow at the same speed all the time, and can be tempered by one's position in or out of its path. The "factor" allows one to suspend one's disbelief for the pleasure it affords.)

When the contents of the film or the decisions of the legislature do not satisfy (i.e., do not still our anxiety, do not offer hope), we elaborate their arid action into a superstory—just as the creation myth is superseded by the pantheon, internecine battles replacing primordial being/nothingness anomie. (If we watch any television drama long enough, the Clinton White House, or *Hill Street Blues*, or *ER*, we will see the original dramatic thrust give way to domestic squabbles. After a while, the new is no longer new, and we require drama. It's how we perceive the world.)

Our survival mechanism orders the world into cause-effect-conclusion.

Freud called music polymorphous perversity. We take pleasure in the music because it states a theme, the theme elaborates itself and then resolves, and we are then as pleased as if it were a philosophical revelation—even though the resolution is devoid of verbal content. Like politics, like most popular entertainment.

Children jump around at the end of the day, to expend the last of that day's energy. The adult equivalent, when the sun goes down, is to create or witness drama—which is to say, to order the universe into a comprehensible form. Our sundown play/film/gossip is the day's last exercise of that survival mechanism. In it we attempt to discharge any residual perceptive energies in order to sleep. We will have drama in that spot, and if it's not forthcoming we will cobble it together out of nothing.

The Perfect Ball Game

What do we wish for in the perfect game?

Do we wish for Our Team to take the field and thrash

the opposition from the First Moment, rolling up a walkover score at the final gun?

No. We wish for a closely fought match that contains many satisfying reversals, but which can be seen, retroactively, to have always tended toward a satisfying and inevitable conclusion.

We wish, in effect, for a three-act structure.

In act 1 Our Team takes the field and, indeed, prevails over its opponents, and we, its partisans, feel pride. But before that pride can mature into arrogance this new thing occurs: Our Team makes an error, the other side is inspired and pushes forth with previously unsuspected strength and imagination. Our Team weakens and retreats.

In act 2 of this perfect game Our Team, shaken and confused, forgets the rudiments of cohesion and strategy and address that made them strong. They fall deeper and deeper into the slough of despond. All contrary efforts seem for naught; and just when we think the tide may have turned back their way, a penalty or adverse decision is rendered, nullifying their gains. What could be worse?

But wait: Just When All Seems Irremediably Lost, help comes (act 3) from an unexpected quarter. A player previously believed second-rate emerges with a block, a run, a throw, that offers a glimmer (a *glimmer*, mind) of the possibility of victory.

Yes, only a glimmer, but it is sufficient to rouse the team to something approaching its best efforts. And the team, indeed, rallies. Our Team brings the score back even and, mirabile dictu, makes That Play that would put them ahead.

ONLY TO HAVE IT CALLED BACK, yet again, by fate, or by its lieutenant, a wrongheaded, ignorant, or malicious official.

But see: the Lessons of the Second Act[1] were not lost on Our Team. This or that one might say it is too late, the clock is too far run down, our heroes are Too Tired, *yet* they rouse themselves for One Last Effort, One Last Try. And do they prevail? Do they triumph, with scant seconds left on the clock?

They *all but* triumph. As, in the final seconds of the play, the outcome rests on That Lone Warrior, that hero, that champion, that person upon whom, in the Final Moment, all our hopes devolve, that final play, run, pass, penalty kick—Yes.

But wait: that Warrior we would have chosen for the

1. We, caught up in the drama of that moment, did not recognize at the time that the second act *had* lessons. We watched and understood it as a series of both random and unfortunate happenings. In *retrospect* we intuit/perceive its operation as part of a whole—i.e., we perceive it as part of a drama.

task, that Champion is injured. No one is left on the bench save a neophyte, et cetera, et cetera.

In which conceit we see that not only does the game recapitulate the drama, but each act of the game (the Perfect Game, mind you) recapitulates the game (following the paradigm: "Yes! No! But wait . . . !"), just as each act of the play recapitulates the whole. The ball game, then, is perhaps a model of Eisenstein's Theory of Montage: the idea of a SHOT A is synthesized with the idea of a SHOT B to give us a third idea, which third idea is the irreducible building block upon which the play will be constructed.

The Defense of Team A and the Offense of Team B are synthesized in THE PLAY, the one play, after which the ball will be found at a different position. And to that new position (a ball in the same position but at a later time is, of course, still in a new position) we, the audience, internalize/intuit/create/assign a philosophical meaning.

For we rationalize, objectify, and personalize the process of the game exactly as we do that of a play, a drama. For, finally, it *is* a drama, with meaning for our lives. Why else would we watch it?

It is enjoyable, like music, like politics, and like theater, because it exercises, it flatters, and it informs our capacity for rational synthesis—our ability to learn a lesson, which is our survival mechanism.

This Play, which May or not Take Place, but which we *perceive* (we can find a similar satisfaction, for example, if we're feeling philosophical, in the interplay of clouds) because we must, because it is our nature, can, at one end of its operation, makes us better, make the world better, perhaps, because of what we have perceived. At the other end of its operation, it can soothe (or, for that matter, enrage and debauch) simply by exciting our capacity for synthesis—as the lovely kitten playing with the ball of string is happy because she practices torture, as patriotic groups are similarly happy because they rehearse—in however embryonic a form—the license of war.

It is difficult, finally, *not* to see our lives as a play with ourselves the hero—and that struggle is the great task of religion, of which drama used to be a part before the Fall.

Anti-Stratfordianism

We, in show business, are told that first this and now that superstar of the stage or screen demands all co-workers sign an agreement not to look at him or her—when the superstar appears, the lowly must avert their gaze.

One musical star now insists that he has no name— just a glyph, or a symbol, and the name is unpronounceable (a distinction heretofore reserved for a certain deity, beloved by my people, the Jews).

Considerable sections of the populace insist that Elvis did not die.

In these cases, the mortal has been raised, or is auditioning to be raised, to the status of a god. Today, as in ancient Rome, when all avenues of success have been traveled and all prizes won, the final prize is the delusion of godhead.

The same grandiosity serves the egos of not only the high but of the low. If voters-viewers-devotées are necessary—in their complicity, if in nothing else—for the act of deification, does that not make *them* greater than a god?

We see the quest for godhead in the affection for the ideas of reincarnation and "channeling." In each the correct-thinking defeat death, that indignity to which the nonelect are unfortunately subject.

The anti-Stratfordians hold that Shakespeare didn't write Shakespeare's plays—it was another fellow of the same name, or of a different name. In this they invert the megalomaniacal equation and make themselves not the elect, but the *superior* of the elect. Barred from composing Shakespeare's plays by a regrettable temporal accident, they, in the fantasy of most every editor, accept the mantle of *primum mobile*, consign the (falsely named) creator to oblivion, and turn to the adulation of the crowd for their deed of discovery and insight—so much more thoughtful and intellectual than the necessarily sloppy work of the writer.

In so doing, the anti-Stratfordians identify themselves as champions of the better-bred (the Earl of Oxford, Bacon, Elizabeth), and, more important, reveal themselves as that-which-conquers-death. They appoint themselves as "eternity"—the force that shall pass on all things.

The assignment of authorship to Bacon, et cetera, is like the sop of management to Lazy Labor—it is on the order of awarding "Best Employee of the Week," in which the true status rests not with the recipient but with the donor, and his or her power to patronize.

The anti-Stratfordian, like the flat-earther and the creationist, elects himself God—possessed of the power to supervene the natural order—and the most deeply hidden but pervasive fantasy of the above is the ultimate delusion of godhead: "*I* made the world."

The Problem Play

The problem play is a melodrama cleansed of invention.

Its stated question, "How do we cure spousal abuse, AIDS, deafness, religious or racial intolerance?" allows the viewer to indulge in a fantasy of power: "I see the options presented, and I decide (with the author) which is correct. Were *I* in the place of those upon the stage, *I* would make the correct choice. And I would vote with the hero or heroine, rather than with the villain."

When (either through the triumph or the ennobling failure of the protagonist), the correct choice is vouch-safed to the audience, its members can, and will, say smugly, "And did I not know it all the time? I *knew* that homosexuals, blacks, Jews, women were people too. And, lo, my perceptions have been proved correct."

That is the reward offered by attendance at the problem play.

The reward offered by the traditional melodrama is some-what different. That melodrama offers anxiety undergone in safety, the problem play offers indignation. (Television news offers both.) In these false dramas we indulge a desire to feel superior to events, to history, in short, to the natural order.

Myth, religion, and tragedy approach our insecurity somewhat differently. They awaken awe. They do not deny our powerlessness, but through its avowal they free us of the burden of its repression.

(The merely ignorant may enjoy Shakespeare's plays. But I would imagine that the anti-Stratfordian's experi-ence of them is never completely untainted by annoy-ance at their false attribution.)

Romance celebrates the inevitable salvation/triumph of the individual over (or through the actions of) the gods—such triumph due, finally, not even to exertion, but to some inherent (if unsuspected) excellence on the part of the protagonist.

Tragedy celebrates the individual's subjugation and thus his or her release from the burden of repression and its attendant anxiety ("when remedy is exhausted, so is grief").

The theater is about the hero journey, the hero and the heroine are those people who do not give in to temptation. The hero story is about a person undergoing a test that he or she didn't choose.

Heroes or heroines in the problem play, however, undergo a test over which they have complete control. They have chosen the test and they are going to succeed. It's a melodrama, and we go along because it makes us feel, to a certain extent, good about ourselves; it's the fulfillment of an adolescent fantasy, like the science fiction film.

We know that at the end of this fantasy good will prevail. We know the Martians will be conquered. We know the hero will discover, in the problem play, that deaf people are also people, that blind people are also people. The villain will be vanquished. The hero will come in and save the girl on the railroad track. And so our enjoyment evaporates the instant we leave the theater. We wanted, like the adolescent, to indulge ourselves in a fantasy of power over the adult world—we did so, and, for the brief moment of the adventure (the stealing of the stop sign) it made us feel powerful.

On the other hand, the hero of a tragedy has to fight the world, though powerless—and with no tools whatever except his will. Like Hamlet or Odysseus or Oedipus or Othello. All hands are turned against these heroes, and they are unfit for the journey they must take. The strength of these heroes comes from the power to resist. They resist the desire to manipulate, the desire to "help." The writer of the Superman comic book, or, for that matter, the government economist can "help" us get to the solution by proclaiming they have suspended natural laws, but finally Hamlet, Othello, and you and I and the rest of the audience have to live in a real world, and the "help" of repression of this knowledge is poor help indeed.

Somebody said (Reagan said it, and I'm sure it was said before him), "The worst nine words in the language are: 'I'm from the government and I'm here to help.' " It means, "I'm going to suggest solutions to a problem in which I'm not only uninvolved but to which I feel superior." It's done by politicians. It's done by teachers and parents.

The children, the voters, the viewers, on hearing of this forthcoming aid, feel hostile but suppress their hostility. They say: "Wait a second, this person is giving me a gift; it's not the gift I wanted, but how dare I feel rage?"

The process of "helping," in the theater, is not participating in the hero journey. It's a process of infantilizing, of manipulating the audience.

The leader, the great man or woman, does not say, "The end justifies the means." The great person says, "There is no end, and even though it may *cost* me (as it cost Saint Joan her life; as it may cost X, Y, or Z the election; as it may cost the actor the audition), I'm not going to give them what they want, if what they want is a lie."

It's the power to resist that affects us. It's the power of someone like Dr. King saying, "I have no tools, you can kill me if you want to, but you will have to kill me."

It's the power of Theodor Herzl, who said, "If you will it, it's not a dream."

Herzl went to the Dreyfus trial and said, "Jews need a homeland, this persecution has got to stop, I'm sorry." And none of the rich would give him money. So he went to the poor and asked them for a dime and a nickel. And everyone said he was a fool. But fifty years later, there's the state of Israel.

The power to resist makes the hero journey affective. And for the audience to undergo that journey, it's essen-

"free," so we can reassure ourselves, again, of what we know to be untrue: that we are superior to circumstance (that we are, in effect, God).

In these—the problem play, the evening news, the romance, the political drama—we have conquered not our nature but our terror, the one specific proposition: we have championed the romantic, which is to say the specious, the fictional, the untrue; and our victory leaves us more anxious than before. If others accept our proclamation of godhead, things in the world must be worse than we imagined, and our anxiety grows. The dictator looks for even less probable ideas to assert, and enforces obedience to them more and more cruelly; the United States searches ludicrously for some just cause in which to triumph; Conan Doyle is forced back to Sherlock Holmes and must rescue him from the Reichenbach Falls.

Our anxious quest for superiority cannot be allayed by momentary triumph. For we know, in the end, we must succumb.

Western European romance gave us Hitler, the novels of Trollope, and the American musical. In each the sometimes hidden but always emerging excellence of the hero wins over all. These dramas may be diverting, but they are false, and have a cumulatively debilitating effect.

We live in an extraordinarily debauched, interesting, savage world, where things really don't come out even.

tial that the writer undergo the journey. That's why writing never gets any easier.

The people who subject themselves to the hero journey come up with the poems of Wallace Stevens or the music of Charles Ives or the novels of Virginia Woolf; or, to put it differently, you can't sing the blues if you haven't had the blues.

Theater is a communal art. One of the best things I know about community is what Saint Paul said: "What I am for you frightens me, but what I am *with* you comforts me. For you, I am a bishop; with you, I am a Christian."

When you come into the theater, you have to be willing to say, "We're all here to undergo a communion, to find out what the hell is going on in this world." If you're not willing to say that, what you get is entertainment instead of art, and poor entertainment at that.

In the problem play, the evening news, the romance, of the *uber*-individual, the eventual triumph is assigned a courtesy position as "in doubt" (the possibility of U.S. victory in the Gulf war; the fate of Sherlock Holmes) to allow us, again, to savor—and overcome—anxiety. But as soon as that installment or that particular war is complete, as soon as "our" victory is proclaimed, the anxiety reasserts itself. We knew it was a false struggle, and we now must cast about for another opponent/another villain/another action film/another oppressed people to

The purpose of true drama is to help remind us of that.

The purpose of true drama is to help remind us of that. Perhaps this does have an accidental, a cumulative social effect—to remind us to be a little more humble or a little more grateful or a little more ruminative.

Stanislavsky says there are two kinds of plays. There are plays that you leave, and you say to yourself, "By God, I just, I never, gosh, I want to, *now* I understand! *What* a masterpiece! Let's get a cup of coffee," and by the time you get home, you can't remember the name of the play, you can't remember what the play was about.

And there are plays—and books and songs and poems and dances—that are perhaps upsetting or intricate or unusual, that you leave unsure, but which you think about perhaps the next day, and perhaps for a week, and perhaps for the rest of your life.

Because they aren't clean, they aren't neat, but there's something in them that comes from the heart, and, so, goes to the heart.

What comes from the head is perceived by the audience, the child, the electorate, as manipulative. And we may succumb to the manipulative for a moment because it makes us feel good to side with the powerful. But finally we understand we're being manipulated. And we resent it.

Tragedy is a celebration not of our eventual triumph but of the truth—it is not a victory but a resignation.

Much of its calmative power comes, again, from that operation described by Shakespeare: when remedy is exhausted, so is grief.

Letters of Transit

That which the hero requires *is* the play. In the perfect play we find nothing extraneous to his or her single desire. Every incident either impedes or aids the hero/heroine in the quest for the single goal.

American political campaigns are, as understood by the attendant hucksters, structured as a drama. The hero is the American People, in the person of the candidate. He or she creates a problem and vows to solve it.

Like the audience of a play, we go along with the gag *not* because we wish the particular problem to be solved (why should we care if Othello murders his imaginary wife?) but because a solution *stands for* the ability of the individual to triumph. Politics is, in effect, a more strictly structured drama than most of those found upon the stage.

Performance art, "happenings," and "mixed media" of the 1960s were a revelation to the artist that the audience would *supply* a plot of its own to the events happening before them between the time the curtain rose and the time it fell, and it was not incumbent on the dramatist/performance artist to do so.

The Gang Comedy, episodic plays, the rash of modular one-act plays drawn to full length—all these are expressions of the revelation that an audience will supply its own plot, as they do in a political campaign. (A *son et lumière* is the reductio ad absurdum of the mechanism, as is a political convention.)

Politics, at this writing, sticks closer to traditional drama than does The Stage itself. A problem is stated, the play begins, the hero (candidate) offers herself as the protagonist who *will* find a solution, and the audience gives its attention.

Like the more traditional drama, the problem in politics is notably imaginary—that is, something that either does not in fact exist or that cannot be eradicated by political action (homosexuals will continue their sexual practices in spite of legislation, women will elect whether or not to terminate a pregnancy irrespective of the laws).

We step onto the car dealer's lot to play out a drama. It is our infrequent opportunity to be made much of, to be courted. We don't want to hear about the design of the engine, we want to hear how smart we are.

And we vote for, and follow with interest, that political hero who dramatizes our lives and relieves, for a while, the feeling of helplessness and anomie that is the stuff of modern civilization.

A car salesman who mocked or ignored our clamor for seduction would starve, as much as he or she was able to speak about things automotive. The politician who addressed legitimately political interests would not last long in office. Who remembers Adlai Stevenson?

So the chimerical, notional quality of the politician's chosen quest reassures us that we are going to get our money's worth (our vote's worth—that we *are*, finally, going to get drama rather than dull reason).

"The future," "Change," "Our Heritage," "Tomorrow," "A Better Life," "The American Way," "Family Values" are dramatic abstractions. They have no referents in reality, and are understood to mean: "When strife is gone. When things have been resolved. When there is no more uncertainty in my life."

The search for witches, Jews, un-Americans, homosexuals, immigrants, Catholics, heretics is, similarly, a pageant and not really a political quest at all. The prime movers elect themselves the protagonists, identify what is causing all that unfortunate uncertainty in the world, and swear to expunge it, if we will just vote for them.[2]

Shakespeare informs us that truth's a dog must be whipped to kennel, while Lady the brach may stand by

---

2. The vote is our ticket to the drama, and the politician's quest to eradicate *fill in the blank* is no different from the promise of the superstar of the summer movie to subdue the villain—both promise us diversion for the price of a ticket and a suspension of disbelief.

the fire and stink. And legitimate political concerns—
the environment, health care—go begging for an audience because they are not dramatic.

The principle of psychic economy operates here, as
in all spheres of our dream life. We may worry all day
about whether to take a vacation in Florida or Utah, but
we aren't likely to dream about it. However much our
quotidian cares consume us, our dreamtime is too valu-
able, and will be devoted to problems not susceptible to
rational consideration.

Our time in the theater is also precious. And the
good play will not concern itself with cares—however
much they occupy us day-to-day—that can be dealt
with rationally.

Drama doesn't need to affect people's behavior.
There's a great and very, very effective tool that changes
people's attitudes and makes them see the world in a new
way. It's called a gun.

Now I've been working with audiences thirty years
or more, in different venues. And I've never met an
audience that wasn't collectively smarter than I am, and
didn't beat me to the punch every time.

These people have been paying my rent, all my life.
And I don't consider myself superior to them and have
no desire to change them. Why should I, and how could
I? I'm no different than they are. I don't know anything

they don't know.

An audience (a populace) can be coerced, by a lie, a bribe (a gun); and it can be instructed/preached at. By anyone with a soapbox and a lack of respect. But in all the above this audience is being abused. They are not being "changed," they are being forced.

Dramatists who aim to change the world assume a moral superiority to the audience and allow the audience to assume a moral superiority to those people in the play who don't accept the views of the hero.

It's not the dramatist's job to bring about social change. There are great men and great women who effect social change. They do so through costly demonstrations of personal courage—they risk getting their heads beat in during the march on Montgomery. Or chain themselves to a pillar. Or stand up to ridicule or scorn. They put their lives on the line, and that can inspire heroism in others.

But the purpose of art is not to change but to delight. I don't think its purpose is to enlighten us. I don't think it's to change us. I don't think it's to teach us.

The purpose of art is to delight us: certain men and women (no smarter than you or I) whose art can delight us have been given dispensation from going out and fetching water and carrying wood. It's no more elaborate than that.

The theater exists to deal with problems of the soul, with the mysteries of human life, not with its quotidian calamities. Eric Hoffer says there's Art, for example, *Waiting for Godot*. And there's popular entertainment—for example, *Oklahoma*. And then there's mass entertainment, like Disneyland. And we sinful creatures, being doomed to death, are probably, given one-billionth of a chance, going to make the bad money drive out the good, going to pervert the beautiful into the debauched and the depraved.

So, while we have and occasionally use the capacity to let art veer toward and partake of that awe in the religion from which it was untimely ripped, so we also have the capacity to pervert these impulses toward the dramatic, to oppress and to enslave each other.[3]

On the one hand, we have Samuel Beckett. On the other hand, we have Leni Riefenstahl. They're both dealing with exactly the same human capacity to order the intolerable into meaning—one creates cleansing art, the other advertisements for murder.

I don't believe reaching people is the purpose of art. In fact, I don't know what "reaching people" means. I

3. Please note that as we exercise these impulses, we do not *say* we wish to "oppress and enslave"—we say we want to "help, teach, and correct." But the end of each is oppression.

know what Hazlitt said: It's easy to get the mob to agree with you; all you have to do is agree with the mob.

Aristotle wrote that no evil can befall a good person either in this life or after death. This pronunciamento can be taken as a jejune promise, or it can, perhaps more correctly, be taken as a definition of evil. That is, whatever befalls the good person, however devastating, cannot be evil if it does not spring from his or her own *actions* (a birth defect may be unfortunate, but it cannot be evil).

Things that can *equally* befall a good or bad person cannot be evil; they can only be accident and, as such, are the fit subject not of drama but of gossip.

Like gossip, "issue" plays have a great capacity to demand our momentary attention; also like gossip, they leave us rather empty after our rush of prurience has run its course and is followed, as it usually is, by shame. And so plays adopt the concerns of politics, the day-to day, while politics adopt the concerns of drama, the creation of myth, filling the theatrical gap.

The presentation of a theatrical objective reassures us that our political attention will be rewarded, just as the presence, in the motion-picture ads in newspapers, of the hero holding a pistol reassures us that we will see "action."

The movie with a gun in the ad and none in the picture will fare as badly as a politician who promises drama and then delivers only social concern. It is therefore essential to the healthy political campaign that the issues be largely or perhaps totally symbolic—i.e. nonquantifiable.

Peace with Honor, Communists in the State Department, Supply Side Economics, Recapture the Dream, Bring Back the Pride—these are the stuff of pageant. They are not social goals; they are, as Alfred Hitchcock told us, *The MacGuffin.* This was, of course, Hitchcock's term for "that which the hero wants," and his devotion to the concept explains much of his success as a film director.

He understood that the dramatic goal is *generic.* It need not be more specific than: the Maltese Falcon, the Letters of Transit, the Secret Documents. It is sufficient for the protagonist-author to know the worth of the MacGuffin. The less specific the qualities of the MacGuffin are, the more interested the audience will be. Why? Because a loose abstraction allows audience members to project their own desires onto an essentially featureless goal. Just as they do onto the terms Americanism, or A Better Life, or Tomorrow.

It is easy to identify with the quest for a secret document, somewhat harder to do so with a heroine whose goal is isolating and understanding the element radium. Which is why in dramatic biography writers and directors end up reverting to fiction. To be effective, the dramatic elements must and finally will take precedence over any "real" biographical facts. We viewers don't care—if we wanted to know about the element radium, we'd read a book on the element radium. When we go to the movies to see *The Story of Marie Curie* we want to find out how her little dog Skipper died.

In a drama, as in any dream, the fact that something is "true" is irrelevant—we care only if that something is germane to the hero-quest (the quest for a MacGuffin) *as it has been stated to us.*

The power of the dramatist, and of the political flack therefore, resides in the ability to state the problem.

(During the O.J. Simpson case I was at a party with a couple of rather famous jurists. I said it occurred to me that a legal battle consisted not in a search for the truth but in jockeying for the right to pick the central issue. They chuckled and pinched me on the cheeks. "You just skipped the first two years of law school," one of them said.)

The Problem, the MacGuffin, the Godless Threat to the Body Politic, these have the power to excite our imagination, and, as Eric Hoffer writes, only by so doing can one control the attention of groups (the mob, the electorate, the audience).

It is the nature of our reasoning faculty to order perceived elements of threat, to identify and structure them so that we can consider alternative methods of overcoming them, and implement the best plan.

That is how we perceive the world. That's what we do all day.

The drama excites us as it recapitulates and calls into play the most essential element of our being, our prized adaptive mechanism.

A puppy who won't respond to the command "come" can and will return to the master if the master falls down and lies still. The puppy will come trotting back. Why? Because it thinks its dominator is incapacitated and it now has a chance to kill. The puppy comes back joyfully, as it is getting a free chance to exercise its most prized survival skills.

Just as we are at the drama. We can exercise our survival skills, racing ahead of the protagonist, feeling vicarious fear while knowing ourselves safe.

That is the power and joy of the drama. That is why the drama that is second-rate, that is not structured as the quest of the hero for a single goal, is forgettable; and that is why dramatic structure, even in nondramatic settings, is such fine entertainment.

CHAPTER TWO
SECOND ACT PROBLEMS

THE problems of the second half are not the problems of the first half.

The journey out always seems longer than the journey back. It is new, and demands our furious concentration as we look for signs, for the characteristic, for the shortcut. On the return we are better able to separate the essential from the extraneous; our concentration has been narrowed to the goal.

So the progression toward the climax, denouement, conclusion accelerates in tempo. We have been given the facts and our attention has narrowed. We now need only remark our progress toward the goal and the occasional incursion of the unusual impediment, the unusual turn of plot.

As the audience has pledged or loaned its attention,

it is easy to interject the extraneous—an audience will accept it as essential until that point at which it has been proved otherwise (that point occurring after the end of the play, as people are on their way home—for which relief they may be counted on to forgive much).

George M. Cohan fixed what he correctly understood to be a first act deficient in interest by having the hero enter, remove a pistol from his coat, look around to make sure he was unobserved, and put the pistol in a bureau drawer.

This introduction of the extraneous is unusual behavior in the first act, where the honeymoon is still in force (it has often been remarked that anyone can write a good first act); but it is not at all uncommon in the *second* act. (A joke from the Algonquin Round Table: A couple of guys are sitting around talking. One says, "How's the play going?" The other says, "I'm having second act problems." Everybody laughs. "Of *course* you're having second act problems!")

When the curtain goes up, we've got your attention. So we dramatists don't *have* to do anything for a while. Later, either the plot will kick in or the audience will start yawning and eating popcorn. It's very common in the second act of a play for an extraneous element to be interjected.

The audience wants to be piqued, to be misled, to be disappointed at times, so that it can, finally, be fulfilled. The audience therefore needs the second act to end with a question.

This is fine for the audience, as they do not need to know, at this point, what the answer to that question is. But the artist must. "Oh lord," the artist says, at this one-third point, "here I find myself neither with the resolve and strength of the beginning nor with the renewal of strength that comes from a sight of the end—here I am, in short, in the middle."

Or the artist says, "It's in my head, are you really going to make me write it down?" Solutions to the problem of the middle act are the test of character.

If artists elect themselves superior to their protagonists, the task is simplicity itself—they manufacture a complication—like Cohan sticking the pistol in the drawer.

To have the end buried in the beginning (which is the utmost accomplishment of drama), however, is a bit more difficult. It means that in the middle term the previously unsuspected must emerge; and, emerging, must sink the protagonist (and the artist) into the slough of despair: "I had prepared for anything but this." Out of this despair must come the resolution to complete the journey.

In his analysis of world myth, Joseph Campbell calls this period *in the belly of the beast*—the time which is not the beginning and not the end, the time in which the artist and the protagonist doubt themselves and wish the journey had never begun. This is the staging ground for the assault on the final goal—the time in which the beginning goal is transmuted into a *higher* goal, in which the *true* nature of the struggle asserts itself.

In the life of the artist this is the period inevitably thought of as "the good old days." It is the time of struggle.

We all have a myth and we all live by a myth. That's what we live for. Part of the hero journey is that the hero (artist/protagonist) has to change her understanding completely, whether through the force of circumstance (which happens more often in drama) or through the force of will (which happens more often in tragedy). The hero must revamp her thinking about the world. And this revamping can lead to great art.

Tolstoy wrote that if you don't undergo this reexamination, this revision, in your thirties, the rest of your life will be intellectually sterile. We correctly identify the advent of this phenomenon as a "midlife crisis" and strive to live through it so that we can return to our previously less troubled state—believing that this state stands between us and any possibility of happiness or success. To the contrary, however, this state is the beginning of a great opportunity. Tolstoy suggested that it was the opportunity to change myth by which one lives; to rethink everything; to ask, "What is the nature of the world?"

The middle term, the second act, the morass of the "midlife crisis" is the period of the *latent* dream.

In the first act the *manifest* dream is brought forth. The hero elects/consigns himself to a struggle: to create a Jewish Homeland, to find the cause of the plague on Thebes, to free the Scottsboro Boys.

In the middle term the high-minded goal has devolved into what seems to be a quotidian, mechanical, and ordinary drudgery: now we are not trying to establish the Jewish Homeland but negotiating a contract with a stationer to supply the paper so that we may write fund-raising letters.

Now we are not trying to determine how to live in a world bereft of our father; we are trying to dispatch two impertinent toadies named Rosencrantz and Guildenstern.

The joke has it: remembering you set out to drain the swamp is hard when you're up to your ass in alligators. And that is the problem of the second act.

The act truly tends toward the goal (which is to lead us to the third act: the culmination of the search, the "high" conflict) when the protagonist accepts the burden of the seemingly commonplace, accepts the drudgery, the necessity of continuing without exuberance or even *interest* in the proceeding. This is the point at which the play really starts to take on momentum. The point at which the hero says, "The gay population supported me because I said I would end discrimination against them in the military, and now I'm going to do it, whether I feel like it or not," at which Othello decides to test Iago's theories, at which Rosa Parks refuses to rise from her seat.

How many times have we heard (and said): Yes, I know that I was cautioned, that the way would become difficult and I would want to quit, that such was inevitable, and that *at exactly this point* the battle would be lost or won. Yes, I know all that, but those who cautioned me *could not* have foreseen the magnitude of the specific difficulties *I* am encountering at this point— difficulties which must, sadly, but I have no choice, force me to resign the struggle (and have a drink, a cigarette, an affair, a rest), in short, to declare failure.

It is the romantic model that entices us to that declaration. In the romance the period of struggles is truncated, formalistic, and capped with the intervention of the Fairy Godmother (the God from the Machine, Santa Claus, the arrival of the cavalry).

The family movie is a romance. The hero-child wants to succeed at some grown-up task—to learn karate, baseball, gymnastics, to win this or that race—and becomes an apprentice to a tutor-master, and is found wanting. The master/Godmother/Godfather applies a magic wand or incantation, and the hero finds he has mastered the difficulty.

These romances are a semireligious formulation based on the preeminence of *faith*. In *The Karate Kid*, *Star Wars*, *A Christmas Carol*, the protagonists are granted their wish when they recognize that they have "all within them."

(The modern cult bestseller *A Course in Miracles*, like most self-help agendas, is reducible to a similar dictum: at the point you recognize you are God, you will be God.)

These romances do away with the quest of the middle term—the problems of the second act—in a way similar to hallucinogens' promise of the key to the universe. They reduce the difficulty of the problem to zero and then reward the individual for solving it.

Marijuana, for example, won't help one determine the correct aspect ratio for the tail structure of an airliner, but if the problem is "what do the colors mean?" the individual may safely attribute his or her solution to the drug.

To stretch the conceit, the problem "Where can I get some more of my drug?" may seem difficult, but not as difficult as "How can I live my life in this disappointing, unpredictable, and at times loathsome world?"

In politics as in drama, the false task, the easy task, is often denominated the difficult and noble quest.

It is easier to throw good money after bad, at times, than to admit one was wrong, misguided, arrogant, foolish. But these are the problems of the second act.

"O! what a rogue and peasant slave am I" is the polar opposite of a misguided persistence in an incorrect course (the search for Peace with Honor, the discovery of a biblical defense of slavery or homophobia).

Our understanding of our life, of *our* drama (and the drama on stage or screen can be nothing other than our understanding of *our* personal drama)—this understanding resolves itself into thirds: Once Upon a Time (narration that enables us to understand the difficulty/desire/goal of the hero), Years Passed (the middle time of struggles); And Then One Day (the inevitable yet unforeseen complication engendered, literally *brought into being*, by the quest of the hero in the middle term—the precipitation into the end struggle—which can be seen as the granting of the hero's wish, engendered in the middle term, for a clear-cut fight which would absolutely resolve the question at hand).

For much of our lives we are mired in an inability to frankly regard the middle term, to admit we have made a wrong turning, to return (so we might think) to the beginning of our struggle for knowledge. We tend to elect, rather, to continue in error. (In *Enemy of the People*, Dr. Stockmann *elected* to save the town by determining the source of water contamination; he could not have foreseen that in the middle period he would have to continue to save the town even though the townspeople wanted to kill him for it.)

It is not natural to embrace these problems. It is not comfortable—it calls upon one to admit one's arrogance in trusting to one's own beloved skills and accomplishments. The romance calls for the hero, at this point, to simply exercise "faith," to act as if the problem did not exist.

The true drama (and especially the tragedy) calls for the hero to exercise will, to *create*, in front of us, on the stage, his or her own character, the strength to continue. It is her striving to understand, to correctly assess, to face her own character (in her choice of battles) that inspires us—and gives the drama power to cleanse and enrich our own character.

This is the struggle of the second act.

Violence

The stoics wrote that the excellent king can walk through the streets unguarded. Our contemporary Secret Service spends tens of millions of dollars every time the president and his retinue venture forth.

Mythologically, the money and the effort are spent not to protect the president's fragile life—all our lives are fragile—but to protect the body politic against the perception that his job is ceremonial, and that for all our attempts to invest it with real power—the Monroe Doctrine, the war powers act, the "button"—there's no one there but us.

It is the notion of emptiness the trappings of state are meant to counterbalance. (One could invert the stoics' perception: a country that is unaware that its leadership is ceremonial, that must protect itself against or suppress that perception, must be unhappy. The work of repression may well create anger, and that anger may well be directed against the Leader, who embodies the untenable thought. And *that* is why the Leader is unsafe in the streets.)

Our Defense Department exists neither to "maintain our place in the world" nor to "provide security against external threats." It exists because we are determined to squander all—wealth, youth, life, peace, honor, everything—to defend ourselves against feelings of our own worthlessness, our own powerlessness.

Our World Position is not tenuous, but our mental balance is. In our devotion to the ideas of our own superiority, we are like compulsive gamblers who destroy themselves by enacting a drama of their own worthlessness. They gamble neither to win or lose but to maintain equilibrium, which they can do only *while gambling*—loss and gain bring into focus the disparity between the gamblers' actions and subconscious, and thus cause unrest.

When they win, these gamblers cannot explain to themselves why they continue. If they gambled for wealth, why does wealth not please them? When they, inevitably, lose, they cannot explain why they gambled in the first place—if it was for wealth, why couldn't they see that the inevitable end was loss? Either result is unbearable, and so these gamblers must retreat to the compulsion, and surrender to illogic and pain in order to protect themselves against revelation.

Our baffling foreign policy similarly reveals a compulsion to engage in strife (either as participant or, if such a position is not available, as mediator, in the hope that mediation will lead to involvement in strife).

This compulsion spares us the trauma of dealing with the irreconcilability of two national drives—the need to confess and the need to brag. We deal with Korea by fighting the Vietnam War, with our national surplus and secure trade position by enacting the S & L tragedy. We, increasingly, cannot bear true peace, or work for it, because in peace we might have to confront the unconscious and unhappy underpinnings of our national character.

The superego is created to arbitrate the functions of the conscious and the unconscious mind. So are neuroses and psychoses, so are the arts. When art functions as the synthesizer, the arbitrator, balance is created. In great art—the Bible, Shakespeare, Bach—the balance is long-lasting. It is not that great art reveals a great truth, but that it stills a conflict—by *airing* rather than rationalizing it. (The repression *is* the neurosis, as Freud said.)

Those arts and pseudoarts that appeal only to the conscious mind do not satisfy. Consider, for example, the problem play. Let's say it's 1914 and women do not have the vote. One young woman, who's committed to women's suffrage, gets all her friends together, and they address the issue. Among these friends is an intelligent woman who nonetheless opposes universal suffrage. So we have a scene between the two women. Then we have a scene between the woman who opposes universal suffrage and her husband. Then we have a scene between two women who support suffrage, one of whom is frightened to endorse it, however, because she once had an affair, and she is afraid that the glare of publicity may bring the affair to light, et cetera.

If you or I start writing that play, like scenes will suggest themselves and we will let them work themselves out. But the play is a product of the conscious mind. It's been overburdened by the necessity of expressing a consciously held view of the world. And the idea of women's suffrage is so important that it has to color everything. Each scene and each line of each scene must tend toward the right conclusion—that women's suffrage is good—and the unconscious mind will never, ever, take part in the creation of this play.

And so we have a very important topic which, nonetheless, cannot be the stuff of art. It might make a good tract, it might make a good political platform, it might make a good speech. But it can't be art.

Brecht wrote about the alienation effect and the agitprop uses of theater. But these writings bear little relationship to his plays, which are extraordinarily charming and beautiful and lyrical and upsetting. *Coincidentally*, they happen to be on social issues. (I think Brecht is a great playwright. I think his theoretical writing is somewhat problematic.)

We may, as at any presentation that assures us of our power and rectitude (flag waving, and so on) shout praise at these pseudoarts, but after the shouting we are empty and alone. Those presentations appeal to our ego. They inform us that everything—understanding, world domination, happiness—is within us, and within our grasp ("We're Number One!"), and that life, for those as powerful, perceptive, and blessed as we, should be and will be simple.

But life is not simple, the truth is not simple, true art is not simple. True art is as deep and convoluted and various as the minds and souls of the human beings who create it.

We may return to the pseudoart again and again, like the compulsive eater or gambler, hoping that *next* time our choice will be correct. But the purpose of compulsion is not a search for peace; it's an enforced strengthening of the compulsion itself. (People are drawn to summer movies because they are *not* satisfying—and so they offer opportunities to repeat the compulsion.)

In endeavoring to elect the perfect leader, in searching for the perfect, biggest-grossing film, in showering with awards the most predictable of diversions, we aim to continue the compulsion. The perfect leader/perfect film does not exist, any more than the winning bet will cure the compulsive gambler. And what we define as the path "toward perfection" exists only to keep us ignorant of our basic imbalance.

To surround the president with hundreds of dedicated shooters, to pay movie stars tens of millions of dollars for three months' work, is not only to propitiate the gods but to propitiate the principals *as* gods—to declare, "*This* time I have found the perfect one. This time I have succeeded."

When we find that we have, inevitably, failed, we suppress our self-loathing by making our standards stricter. We repress our anger at our failure to choose correctly.

But the anger expresses itself in images of violence.

The film car chase and even the cry "there is too much violence in the films" reveal this: art, the organic medium for arbitration between the conscious and subconscious, has been pressed into service of the compulsion mechanism itself. Art, no longer the province of the artist, has become the tool of the entrepreneur—which is to say, the tool of the conscious mind. The conscious mind asks, "What is art good for?" and responds, "It is good for pleasing people."

But the conscious mind can derive no enjoyment from pleasing people through art, for the conscious mind cannot create art. So the conscious mind allies itself to art, and derives enjoyment from making money.

(Please note that the altruistic "I will help people, I will bring art to them" and the venal "if I give them what they want, I will be rich" are equivalent misuses of the human need for art. They are both exploitative. In neither case is the need for art being met; in both cases the individual gets satisfaction from participating in the mechanism.)

Artists don't wonder, "What is it good for?" They aren't driven to "create art," or to "help people," or to "make money." They are driven to lessen the burden of the unbearable disparity between their conscious and unconscious minds, and so to achieve peace.

When they create art, their nonrational synthesis has the power to bring *us* peace. The words of the rational mind have no power to bring us peace through art. (We may all display the American flag without increasing our sense of national security—in fact, it is fairly clear that the visibility of the flag's display is directly proportional to our *insecurity*.)

The artist has to undergo the same hero struggles as the protagonist. If you're sitting in the writers' building on the Fox lot and getting paid $200,000 a week, you know that you'd better stop daydreaming and start coming up with *Benji: The Return*.

But if you're sitting all by yourself in the coffee shop, smoking that cigarette, you're much freer to follow your own bizarre, troubling thoughts. Because all of your thoughts, at bottom, are bizarre and troubling. (If they weren't, not only wouldn't we go to the theater, we wouldn't dream.) So there you sit in the coffee shop, talking to yourself. "Oh my God, is this the real thing? Has someone thought of this before? Am I insane? Is anybody going to like it?"

That's part of the process too. And it's probably a sign that you're on the right track. I used to say that a good writer throws out the stuff that everybody else keeps. But an even better test occurs to me: perhaps a good writer keeps the stuff everybody else throws out.

Most traumatic for young and idealistic students of art is the knowledge (if and when they can face it) that their idealism is absolutely useless. The reasonable person might conclude, "Art is what people want. Give them what they want." But what you and I want from art is peace. The producer, the entrepreneur, the foundation person, cannot know that; the *artist* doesn't even know it. He or she is, simply, driven. Artists don't set out to bring *anything* to the audience or to anyone else. They set out, again, to cure a raging imbalance.

The reasonable entrepreneur sets out to "give the people what they want." And reason suggests they want thrills and mutilation. They want violence. But the immense success of trash speaks not to its value as art, or even as entertainment, but to its function as a form of repression. Las Vegas doesn't offer fortune (though it purports to) or thrills (unless one finds degradation thrilling). It offers the opportunity to exercise one's compulsion.

Violence is not entertaining per se. Our endorsement of violence in art, like our endorsement of violence in our nation's behavior, is a compulsive expression of the need to repress—to identify a villain and destroy it. The compulsion must be repeated because it fails. It fails because the villain does not exist in the external material world. The villain, the enemy, is our own thoughts.

The public endorses these entertainments subconsciously. The viewer returns to them because they do *not* work—and so he must try again, first propitiating the gods with increased fervor, more money, more devotion, more attention.

But we cannot gamble enough to find peace, eat enough to be thin, arm ourselves and strut enough to feel secure.

Racist America elected African Americans The Villain. Once elected, that race suffered not because it was the cause of the whites' unrest, but because it was *not*.

Christian Europe elected Jews the cause of its distress, and fury against the Jews mounted as each pogrom proved unrewarding. Anti-Semitism flourishes today in Germany, a country virtually devoid of Jews.

As our center disintegrates, the electronic media rise and centralize to ensure their utility as a means of oppression. Art, which exists to bring peace, becomes entertainment, which exists to divert, and is becoming totalitarianism, which exists to censor and control. The desire to express becomes, absent the artist and in the face of the terrifying, the need to repress. The "information age" is the creation, by the body politic, through the collective unconscious, of a mechanism of repression, a mechanism that offers us a diversion from our knowledge of our own worthlessness.

Self-Censorship

The avant-garde is to the left what jingoism is to the right. Both are a refuge in nonsense. The warm glow of fashion on the left and patriotism on the right evidence individuals' power to elect themselves members of a group superior to reason.

In endorsing a blank canvas, or the Domino Theory, the individual becomes like a King Canute, happy to bid the sea stop, a being not bound by natural forces.

The election of a dictator is a form of self-censorship; for, as Tolstoy points out, five million men did not march into Russia because Napoleon willed it. The mysterious process of war and politics must conceal a deep herd or genetic tropism, a force so strong and inexplicable that the individual, to maintain autonomy, must explain it as reason—or, in the case of war, as patriotism.

And so the herd, or the gene pool, culls and redistributes population (and information); and the dictator, the dictatorial force (i.e., right-thinking people), protects the prerogatives of the tropism by discouraging independent thought, nonconformity, art. This discouragement, censure, imprisonment, torture, or death may be, in the totalitarian state, blamed on the Dictator, but it must finally be a deep necessity of the Mob, of the requirements of the macro-organism.

We have seen art in a totalitarian culture. Communist bloc theater directors, in that era, staged innocuous classics in a "style" that could be understood by the audience as derogatory to authority.

The same mechanism, called sniping from cover, can be seen in the blank canvases of the 1970s, in action painting, in the wrapping of buildings and natural phenomena in plastic, in performance and video "art." These activities are rather meaningless as art. They do, however, have the power to marshal the individual's need for release/completion, while not threatening his or her psychic or physical integrity. The Secret Police aren't going to come in the night and drag away the director who set *Hamlet* in the Second Stomach of a

Cow and dressed the actors as enzymes; the stockbroker is not going to lie awake worrying about truths or questions raised by a framed canvas painted one shade of green (which is why he or she purchased it).

In this so-called art we see the operations of a self-censorship, of a censorship like that of a totalitarian state (benign, nonphysical, of course, but revealing the same human wish to be controlled and to call such desire autonomy).

As our Western-American world culture completes its manifest destiny, we see literacy, colloquy, education eroding, just as in another form of totalitarian state.

The Germans created and accepted Nazi domination in the name of self-determination; we create and accept ignorance and illiteracy in the name of information.

A television with seven hundred channels of "choice" is not freedom but coercion. The machine we have created demands to be watched; it bleats at us, "There is *nothing* I will not do to hold your attention." We vote for lobotomized immobility and call it entertainment. Why? It is as illogical as the Vietnam War, the Belgian Orphans, Supply-Side Economics, "Happenings."

That we call our intellectual and cultural impoverishment reasonable is mysterious. It must therefore cloak a deeper necessity.

For this censorship-through-information seems to be, like war, an intellectual hibernation, the mass equivalent of an antipsychotic drug, the exercise wheel in the hamster cage—a self-administered anesthesia.

Years ago, I was watching a film at a small theater in Vermont. In the film the hero is chopping wood. He picks up a gnarled, knotty piece, puts it on the block, and raises the maul over his head. The audience, as one, gave a chuckle-sigh-groan: that piece is not going to want to split, they knew it. Not because they'd seen in on TV, but because they'd had that experience. In the theater they were brought, unconsciously, to share the experience with one another, brought closer to one another, into a *community*. They saw what they all knew to be true, and shared what they knew, and discovered with each other that they all knew it to be true, and That Was The Way Life Was. Is this a picayune example?

The same mechanism functions when we watch Shakespeare and listen to "the proud man's contumely . . . the law's delay"; when we hear Willy Loman say, "He's liked, but he's not *deeply* liked"; when we see Dr. Stockmann reviled for trying to do his job; when we hear the unutterable truths of a Bach fugue; when we stand next to each other and look at a Turner sunset. How often have we said, "Wish you were here to share it with me"?

We don't say that of a television program. The purpose of "information" is not to share truths but to immobilize and enervate the mind.

David Halberstam gave a commencement speech I was privileged to hear. He asked the graduating class to consider that the most successful students had been offered jobs as consultants. The jobs carried large salaries because the position of "consultant" was not one to which a twenty-year-old would normally aspire unless he were bribed—there was nothing intrinsically interesting in such a job, so it *had* to be attended by a large paycheck. It was not the sort of thing that a young, energetic person would occupy herself with unless bribed.

Mass media, similarly, are created (by what force we cannot say); they spring into existence, if you will, and offer the promise, in many cases the reality, of great wealth to entice talented people who would otherwise be uninterested. They offer, like any other dictator, the promise of freedom if applicants consign themselves to slavery.

The writer, the actor, the director, no less than the viewer, are thus wooed to spend their lives doing nothing. They are paid handsomely (or merely promised handsome payment, the lure of wealth being so potent that a promise is often sufficient—like the gold rush or the lottery—to hold the multitude). They are paid to remove themselves from the ranks of potential artists, to give up the desire to express, confront, connect, mourn, question, decry, unite; they are paid to serve the cause of censorship.

I remember being told in school that art flourished during times of abundance, which allowed the culture, and the individual, to rise above the claims of subsistence and gave them, in effect, a surplus with which to create.

It seems to me, however, that the opposite is true. In the life of the individual and in the life of the community or the culture, art flourishes in times of struggle, and, in times of surplus, disappears.

The Artist looks back with love on the Powers of his or her salad days, the Theater of the Depression, the Cinema in the Early Days, the cabaret stage. Age, comfort, subsidy, and surplus dull the need and so the ability to speak out. And art is an expression of that *need*. It is not an elective operation. To consider it as such is folly and self-censorship.

A one-hour flying visit to the Louvre is not an experience of Art (it barely even qualifies as "Art Appreciation," that scholastic nonsense of my youth). Now consider a museum with millions of "experiences," and those not masterpieces but advertisements. That is what we find on the seven hundred channels of video.

What right-thinking individual would spend hours, *hours* every evening, watching advertisements? Is it not clear that a product which must spend fortunes drawing attention to itself is probably not one we need?

In watching the television, in buying the product, we endorse the expenditure, we silently worship the idea of wealth, the idea of a state beyond strife—like the commoner who is unable to stop calling the duchess "My Lady."

We will not encounter art in information any more than we will find love in the arms of a prostitute. And we know it. Information, the destructive countervailing force, travels under the mantle of art, or its more humble simulacrum, entertainment, as rapine and pillage go by the name Lebensraum or Manifest Destiny or the Monroe Doctrine.

We are, in the grip of this phenomenon, entering a new dark age. The information age is centralizing knowledge, rendering it liable to despotic control. We can write letters and deliver them by hand. If, however, we communicate only over the phone lines, the flip of one centralized switch renders us isolated.

Similarly, if "information" is centralized in government-controlled "computer banks," liable to power outage or any electronic mishap, might one not intuit that, yet again, the culture is voting for/being impelled toward an *eradication* of knowledge?

Yet again, we are in the sway of vast forces—forces so vast, their sweep so difficult to resist, that we must explain their power over us by fervently advocating them, by defining their unquestionable, irresistible power as financial cornucopia and, by extension, as "good."

In entertainment, we, as a culture, change from communicants to consumers. We become like the terrible supermarket test groups so beloved of the Hollywood minds: empowered judges, accountable to no one, passing on each moment of each presentation—thumbs up or thumbs down.

We publish the grosses of motion pictures as news. Might we not next publish the current quote of paintings, to assure us of our correctness in granting them a moment of our time? To a certain extent, we already do this by sticking them in a museum.

The demand of immediate gratification is death for any art which takes place over time (drama, music, dance). That the audience be teased, disappointed, reassured, frightened, and finally freed is the essence of dramatic/ musical form. It has to take place over time, and it must contain reversals. And the greater the art the more upsetting, provoking, "dramatic" those reversals are—it is only, and necessarily, garbage that "makes us feel good all the time."

A G minor 11th means nothing in itself. It's a jumble of notes. Even given a key of B flat, it means little more. We don't know what it "means" until we hear its place in a particular composition.

Just so with the phrase "I love you," just so with the "recognition scene" or the "death scene." A temporal art demands the attention of the individual over time—an individual content to be piqued, to doubt, to be misled, to mourn, to, finally, consign herself to a *process*.

In this process the viewer goes through the same journey as the protagonist—which is, by the way, the same journey as the author.

Just as commercial pabulum reduces all of us (the creator, the "producer," the viewer) to the status of consumer slaves, so dramatic art raises the creators and the viewers to the status of communicants. We who made it, formed it, saw it, went through something together, now we are veterans. Now we are friends.

How different from the drugged individuals sitting in front of flickering television screens, trying to explain the lunacy of their activity to themselves by calling it entertainment or "becoming informed."

CHAPTER THREE

3 USES OF THE KNIFE

IT is an attractive notion, and it may be coincidentally true, that aesthetic norms naturally recapitulate organic processes of perception or creation. That the golden mean of the picture frame, the Parthenon, the 35mm lens reiterates the organic imaginative processes of the brain; that we see in our mind's eye a face in that horizontal frame, or a face and torso, when the frame is turned vertically; or a two-shot, in the 1:1:33 ratio of early films and television. That the full-figure rendition of the human form presupposes, in the horizontal, something for him or her to turn to—another person, an animal, a task—in order to "fill the frame."

That, finally, we close our eyes and "see" in a format approximating the golden mean.

Similarly, in English, we speak colloquially, in iambic pentameter: "I'm going down to the store to buy the cheese," "I told him, but he didn't hear a word," "I swear I'll love you till the day I die," "not now, not later, never. Is that clear?"

If we listen we can hear people in a dialogue complete the iambic line for each other.

"I saw him on the street."

"And what'd he say?"

"He said leave him alone."

"And what'd you say?"

"What do you think I said?"

"Well, I don't know."

Dramatic structure is, similarly, an exercise of a naturally occurring need or disposition to structure the world as thesis/antithesis/synthesis.

Huddie Ledbetter, also known as Leadbelly, said: You take a knife, you use it to cut the bread, so you'll have strength to work; you use it to shave, so you'll look nice for your lover; on discovering her with another, you use it to cut out her lying heart.

The murderer says to himself, in justification, the reason I was working so hard was to have the strength to buy her something nice, that's the reason I rose in the morning, and that's the reason I ate—to have the strength to go to work. That's the reason I shaved my face—to look nice for her. And when she betrayed me, I used the same knife to ensure she gave her love to no one else.

So the dramatist, the blues writer in us, seizes upon the knife as both embodying and witnessing the interchange, subtly changing its purpose through the course of the drama. The knife becomes, in effect, congruent to the bass line in music. For the bass line, not the melody, gives music strength, and moves us. The treble may be pretty, but it is incomplete dramatically unless coupled with the driving inevitability, the drive-to-resolution, that is the bass. The inevitability, the revelation of the deep meaning of the ordinary (the ordinary being the treble), gives Bach's music its power. The fugues, the toccatas, the greatest of all Western music are affecting as the bass line is affecting.

The tragedy of murder is affecting as the irony of the recurrent knife is affecting. The appearance of the knife is the attempt of the orderly, affronted mind to confront the awesome; to discover the hidden structure of the word. In this endeavor our rational mind will not be of help. This is the province of theater and religion.

Most great drama is about betrayal of one sort or another. Somebody came up to Arthur Miller after an opening and said, "That was a nice play, but couldn't you call it *Life of a Salesman*?" But a play is not about nice things happening to nice people. A play is about rather terrible things happening to people who are as nice or not nice as we ourselves are.

The Russians say: laughing bride, weeping wife/ weeping bride, laughing wife. The couple who write their own marriage ceremony have, we can predict, a rocky time ahead.

This supposed ability to sidestep, to forgo, ritual comes from a mistaken belief in one's own powers and a misapprehension of personal grace. It is misplaced and it is sad, like the viewer at a magic show who confides, "You know, he really didn't make that duck disappear."

Now of course the magician didn't make that duck disappear. What he did was something of much greater worth—he gave a moment of joy and astonishment to some who were delighted by it.

In suspending their disbelief—in suspending their reason, if you will—for a moment, the viewers were rewarded. They committed an act of faith, or of submission. And like those who rise refreshed from prayers, their prayers were answered. For the purpose of the prayer was not, finally, to bring about intercession in the material world, but to lay down, for the time of the prayer, one's confusion and rage and sorrow at one's own powerlessness.

So the purpose of the theater is not to fix the social fabric, not to incite the less perceptive to wake up and smell the coffee, not to preach to the converted about the delights (or the burdens) of a middle-class life. The purpose of theater, like magic, like religion—those three harness mates—is to inspire cleansing awe.

The young intellectual says, "Why go to the wake, why go to the funeral, why parrot some traditional wedding vows? I have nothing to say at the wake, nothing I could say could make a difference at the Shiva, and the archaic wedding ceremony doesn't apply to me."

This is not wisdom but human ignorance, and a kind of personal idolatry. Of *course*, the individual is powerless when confronted by death—whatever would have led him or her to think otherwise? The presence at the Shiva, at the wake, is not and is not meant to be a denial. It is a *confession* of powerlessness in the face of death; and in pleading reason as an excuse, one misses the point entirely.

We all know the hard-bitten rationalist who rails against religious tradition, against the historical niceties, against participation in ritual large and small—the PTA, the Welcome Wagon, the wedding, the funeral. We all know this person, and many of us are this person, and some of us are this person at some times. This person may go to the grave lonely, angry, and drained by resistance to observations and activities, subscription to which would have occupied a fraction of her energy and time.

The heresy of the Information Age is not even that reason will triumph, but that reason *has* triumphed. But reason, as we see in our lives, is employed one thousand times as casuistic rationale for the one time it may be used to further understanding.

And the cleansing lesson of the drama is, at its highest, the worthlessness of reason.

In great drama we see this lesson learned by the hero. More important, we undergo the lesson ourselves, as we have *our* expectations raised only to be dashed, as we find that we have suggested to ourselves the wrong conclusion and that, stripped of our intellectual arrogance, we must acknowledge our sinful, weak, impotent state—and that, having acknowledged it, we may find peace.

The Eleven O'Clock Song

It is common, in romantic films, to encounter the montage. In the romantic film "montage" means a film essay without dialogue, usually accompanied by sentimental music.

This use of the term has nothing to do with its original meaning, as suggested by Eisenstein. Originally the term meant the juxtaposition of two disparate and uninflected images in order to create in the mind of the viewer a third idea, which would advance the plot. (A man who's walking down the street turns his head and reaches tentatively in his pocket; shot of a store window with a sign that says SALE; the viewer thinks, "Oh, that man would like to buy something.") The first idea juxtaposed with the second idea makes the viewer—us—create the third idea.

In the romantic film, montage does not always advance the plot—usually does not, in fact, advance the plot—but rather narrates the supposed mental/emotional state of the protagonist, without dialogue, with music, by repeating slightly different renditions of the same idea.

The hero of the triste romance "reminisces" about his "loss" (dissatisfaction, absent love). He "remembers" (the camera shows) a hotel lobby, two people checking in; a scene on a beach at twilight; a droll occurrence at a restaurant. These scenes are repetitive rather than progressive. There is usually no good reason for one to precede or to follow another. They are not an inevitable progression, they are simply arranged prettily. It is, in fact, an identifying characteristic of this montage that it can be restructured ad-lib—a condition foreign to drama, a feature of the epic rather than the dramatic form.

The film *Bad Day at Black Rock* is a superb drama—an excellently structured and executed dramatic thriller. At one point, however, Spencer Tracy, the hero, begins to narrate his reasons for coming to Black Rock, and his emotional state "before the story began," and how, because of the "story," that state has changed. This scene, a blot on an otherwise superb film, is the equivalent of the emotional montage.

We don't care about the hero's state "before the story began," and we didn't miss hearing how he felt or feels about himself before he vouchsafed the information.[1]

Like the emotional montage, this speech is accepted by the audience in good faith, but without interest. Because it is a solution for which there is no problem, the answer to a question we didn't ask, it is foreign to the dramatic form.

This speech, this montage in film or on stage, I've come to call "The Death of My Kitten." It often contains the phrase or the idea "I don't know why I'm telling you all this."

Why, in a drama, would a character (by definition a character in a drama is engaged in an exacting pur-

1. If we are to identify with the Hero, which is to say, to see her story as our own, she can have *had* no "state" before the beginning of the story. For our journey to be *her* journey, it must begin at the same time.

suit—Aristotle says the character *is* that pursuit), why would this character speak for no good reason? And yet this moment is a feature of much drama and some tragedy.

"I don't know why I'm telling you this . . ." is one way to identify such a montage. Alternatively: "You know, years ago . . ." or "When I was young . . ." or "Once upon a time I had a kitten . . ." and shots of people with their arms spread, twirling in slow motion on a beach.

Not only does this unneeded narration occur regularly in plays and film, it occurs in approximately the same place: seven-tenths of the way through, just before or just after the beginning of the third act. Why?

It is the excrudescence of a naturally occurring process which cannot be directly perceived, but which must be inferred because of its effects.

If something cannot be explained as a problem, perhaps we should try explaining it as a solution.

I began to wonder if this anomaly were a function of our consciousness, a natural by-product of the way we perceive events. Dramatic structure is not an arbitrary—or even a conscious—invention. It is an organic codification of the human mechanism for ordering information. Event, elaboration, denouement; thesis, antithesis, synthesis; boy meets girl, boy loses girl, boy gets girl; act one, two, three.

There's a parable by Tolstoy about a man who was very, very poor. He had three small loaves of bread and a little pretzel. And he came home from working in the fields and he ate a loaf of bread. He was still hungry. So he ate the second loaf of bread and was still hungry. He ate the third loaf of bread. Then he ate the pretzel and was full. He said, "What an idiot I am. I should have eaten the pretzel first."

That's the way our minds work. The human mind cannot create a progression of random numbers. Years ago computer programs were designed to do so; recently it has been discovered that they were flawed—the numbers were not truly random. Our intelligence was incapable of creating a random progression and therefore of programming a computer to do so.

We do not perceive randomness. In the absence of phenomena made significant by being directed toward itself, the infant will order unrelated events into a dramatic whole (a whole comprehensible under the rules of drama), and this is called Neurosis or Psychosis.

We look at our friends who've announced their surprise separation, and we remember their courtship, culminating in the wedding; their early married years, ending in the birth of the first child; and that state of supposed completion, ending in the announcement of their divorce. Later we might think of courtship/marriage/the New Inamorata, and the drama will once again be reordered to conform to the three-act mode of thesis, antithesis, synthesis.

It is our nature to elaborate perception into hypotheses and then reduce those hypotheses to information upon which we can act. It is our special adaptive device, equivalent to the bird's flight—our unique survival tool. And drama, music, and art are our celebration of that tool, exactly like the woodcock's manic courting flight, the whale's breaching leap. The excess of ability/energy/skill/strength/love is expressed in species-specific ways. In goats it is leaping, in humans it is making art.

I began to wonder if this seven-tenths phenomenon were indicative of a human need. What purpose could it serve? What need did its presence reveal? In the drama it seems a vitiation of the play's strength, of the unswerving progress toward the one end—the single goal of the hero. That emotional montage that puts the audience to sleep.

What might it mean?

We begin, or are about to begin, the third act.

The hero and the audience (as allied participants) have "signed on" for the most difficult part of the journey. The stakes have been raised, the possibility of withdrawal has been removed, all is eagerness or dread, and yet we pause. We stop like the travelers in the Russian play: packed for the journey, the conveyance just outside, we turn from the door and sit a while.

In the drama, the clunky and amateurish set piece occurring here stops us for a while and explains itself to us. "When I was young I had a kitten." "You know, before I got myself into this mess I used to think . . ." And: "I don't know why I'm telling you this." Could this speech be the survival of the soliloquy?

It has been said that a poem is never completed; it is only abandoned. Like a poem, a drama is difficult to structure. In my experience the dramatist gets tired at precisely the same point as the protagonist: facing the third act. The act is outlined, the task is plain, if difficult, and the very clarity of the task is dispiriting.

Once the third act is planned, for better or worse, the play is done. Dramatists complete the act with whatever gifts of dialogue and invention they have been given, but the die is cast. The potter has fired the piece. Still, the act has to be written (the pot still has to be glazed), and the dramatist thinks, again, "Oh, come on—it's in my head. Must I go on? Are you really going to make me write it down?"

Tiger-by-the-tail, stakes-raised-almost-out-of-recognition . . . the dramatist and the protagonist, facing the third act, are weary.

Because of their weariness, an anachronism asserts itself.[2] Perhaps this seven-tenths position is a race memory that "holds the place" of the soliloquy; this memory must run back to the antique drama and, before that, to the religious observances from which it evolved.

For the soliloquy is essentially a confession.

In its survival the dramatist/protagonist confesses powerlessness in the face of the gods/the ways of the stage/existence.

It reaches its height in Shakespeare's Crispin Crispian Day speech and degenerates into "The Death of My Kitten." It is found in the positioning of the final pas-de-deux or duet before the concluding massiveness of the ballet or opera. And it is found in the "eleven-o'clock song," that staple of musical comedy, that wistful emotional offering calculated to prime the audience for the trip home.

Why did the soliloquy/confession/profession—which is the protagonist talking to God—die out? Perhaps, with the beginning of widespread literacy, it split off from the drama, as the drama split off from religious

2. My father had a lisp as a child, and, like Demosthenes, he cured himself. And he went on to become a magnificent advocate and speaker. When he was tired, the lisp came back. When they first made automobiles, they put a whip holder up front—a survival from horse-and-buggy days.

celebration and survives in the more leisurely epic form, as the novel.

And perhaps, if these surmises are true, they suggest something about the autonomic nature of the evolution of the drama.

The End of the Play

Much of our communal life seems to be a lying contest: the courts, politics, advertising, education, entertainment. Tolstoy said it is an error to speak of "in these days." So, though I would like to aver that our day is particularly corrupt, I must bow to his wisdom and say, it (and you and I) were ever thus.

If it is our nature, as a society, as human beings, men and women, your nature and mine, to lie, to love to lie, to lie to others, to lie to ourselves, and to lie about whether we lie—if this is our nature, where does the truth emerge?

Perhaps in that final moment when the murderer can admit his crime, the politician her malfeasance, the husband and wife their infidelities. And perhaps not even then.

Religion offers the cleansing mechanism of confession: the Catholic confessional, the Jewish Day of Atonement, the Baptist Testimony. Twelve-step programs are built upon, and proceed from the confession of powerlessness. In all of these we lay our burden down—or we are offered that choice.

For it is not the things we do that injure us, as Mary McCarthy said, it is what we do after them.

And we have created the opportunity to face our nature, to face our deeds, to face our lies in The Drama. For the subject of drama is The Lie.

At the end of the drama THE TRUTH—which has been overlooked, disregarded, scorned, and denied—prevails. And that is how we know the Drama is done.

It is done when the hidden is revealed and we are made whole, for we *remember*—we remember when the world was upset. We remember the introduction of That New Thing that unbalanced a world we previously thought to be functioning well. We remember the increasingly vigorous efforts of the hero or heroine (who stands only for ourselves) to rediscover the truth and restore us (the audience) to rest. And, in the good drama, we recall how each attempt (each act) seemed to offer the solution, and how raptly we explored it, and how disappointed we (the hero) were on finding we had been wrong, until:

At the End of the Play, when we had, it seemed, exhausted all possible avenues of investigation, when we were without recourse or resource (or so it seemed), when we were all but powerless, all was made whole. It was made whole when the truth came out.

At that point, then, in the well-wrought play (and perhaps in the honestly examined life), we will understand that what seemed accidental was essential, we will perceive the pattern wrought by our character, we will be free to sigh or mourn. And then we can go home.

INDEX

PN 1631 .M26 1998
OCLC 37115843
3 uses of the knife /
Mamet, David.

DATE DUE